To Shea, Meghan & Brendan

Barbara J. Ness

The Singing Mouse

Written by: Barbara J. Ness

Illustrated by: Donna Merchant

Requests for permission to make copies of any part of the work
should be mailed to the following address:
2DonnBooks
11354 Links Drive
Reston, Virginia 20190

Published by 2DonnBooks, United States in 2006
Graphic layout: Catherine Hebert
Editor: Francie Donnell
Consulting Editor: Peggy Storch
Printed in China by TSE WORLDWIDE PRESS

Ness, Barbara J.

The Singing Mouse

Author: Barbara J. Ness
Illustrator: Donna Merchant
First U.S. edition 2006

p.cm. Summary:
A charming story of a little country mouse whose talent for
singing leads to wonderful new friendships.

[1. Mouse – Fiction, Singing - Fiction] I. Merchant, Donna II. Title
All characters in this story are fictitious.
Ages K through 5th grade.

ISBN 09770893-1-2
First U.S. Edition 2006

2DonnBooks
11354 Links Drive
Reston, Virginia 20190

Dedicated with heartfelt thanks to the following:

My sister Jane, who got things started.

My sister Sally, my right hand, handling correspondence, typing and archiving my work.

My husband Stan, my caregiver and encourager.

Our children, grandchildren, siblings and extended family, who help where they can.

The people at 2DonnBooks, especially Donna Merchant, for her delightful illustrations, and Francie Donnell, for taking a chance on an unknown.

And to my loving Heavenly Father, who brought all the pieces together. –B.J.N.

To Paul for your enthusiasm and encouragement, and to Ben for your magical hugs, grins, giggles and patience while Mommy drew her pictures. Love always –D.M.

In a kitchen drawer in a country house
There lived a little singing mouse.
A singing mouse? You should have heard!
He sounded very much like a bird.

But, since it was an empty house,
No one was there to hear this mouse.
That was a sad way for things to be,
Because he sang so prettily.
There aren't many mice with a voice for song,
So not being heard was certainly wrong.

And then one day, through a hole in the door,
A toad came hopping across the floor.

"Pardon me," said the toad, when he saw the mouse,
"I thought this was an empty house.
I surely didn't mean to intrude.
Forgive me for being so very rude."

"You are most welcome in my house.
I'd like you to stay," said the singing mouse.
"And if you have a minute or two,
I will sing a song for you."

A singing mouse? Thought the gentleman toad.
That's something I wouldn't hear out on the road.
He listened to the mouse's song,
Then said that he had to be hopping along.

"My good mouse," he said, "I like hearing you sing.
I have some friends I would like to bring.
I know they'd enjoy such a beautiful song.
May I come back, and bring them along?"

"Oh, bring them, please do,"
said the singing mouse.
"It will be fun to have guests in the house."

The toad hopped off through the hole in the door,
And the mouse practiced singing like never before.
He practiced the high notes and practiced the low.
He sang every tune 'til he had it just so.

He cleaned up the house with a little straw broom.
He put some chairs in the very best room,
And lined them all up in a row,
So everyone could see the show.

It was a happy little mouse
Who welcomed his guests into the house.

A sparrow came, and a chipmunk, too;
A big raccoon and a tiny shrew.

A possum with a pinkish nose,
A mourning dove with pinkish toes.

A squirrel with his tail held tall,
And a bunny with almost no tail at all.

The toad hopped in with two of his brothers
And sat right down with all the others.
At last the show was underway,
And, oh, it was a glorious day!

The little mouse just loved to sing,
And singing for friends was a wonderful thing.
First came a silly song for fun:
"Three Blind Mice. See how they run!"

Then a lullaby, soft and sweet;

And a Sousa march for tramping feet.

The soaring notes of "Danny Boy."
Ludwig von Beethoven's "Ode to Joy."

And for a rousing curtain call,
He sang "The Wabash Cannonball."

The audience gave a round of applause
(As best you can with wings and paws.)

The singing mouse bowed; then everyone stayed
To have some cake and lemonade.

They all agreed it was such fun,
Each Thursday now, at half-past one,

They all come back to the country house
To hear the little singing mouse.

And, if you're lucky, someday you

May hear a little mouse singing, too.

Barbara J. Ness, a graduate of Wartburg College in her hometown of Waverly, Iowa, has had a passion for creative writing and storytelling since childhood. After college, she pursued a career as a teacher and a librarian, and spent more than 10 years sharing her love of writing and literature with hundreds of kindergarten, first and second grade students.

The Singing Mouse is Barbara's first published story and is the culmination of an idea based on the memory of an actual singing mouse that had taken up residence in her childhood home.

Although she was diagnosed with ALS (Lou Gehrig's Disease) in 2004 and continues to face many challenges, Barbara remains energized and focused on her craft. Her hope is that her own writing will allow children to experience the kind of spontaneous and joyful pleasure she so often saw mirrored on the faces of her young students as she read to them.

Barbara lives with her husband Stan in Minneapolis, Minnesota. They have four children and eleven grandchildren.

Donna Merchant, a children's book illustrator originally from Powhatan, Virginia, earned a Bachelor of Fine Arts degree from Virginia Commonwealth University. She taught art to children in kindergarten through middle school for nine years at a private school in Fairfax, Virginia. In 2005, Donna published her first illustrated book, *Goblins Will Be Seen When It's Time For Halloween.* Currently, she enjoys being a stay-at-home mom, while continuing to pursue new creative projects with 2DonnBooks.

The Singing Mouse is Donna's first collaboration with writer Barbara Ness. The inspiration for the illustrations comes from her life-long love of animals.

Donna lives with her husband Paul and her four-year-old son Benjamin in Dale City, Virginia.